EXTREME SUPERCARS

PAUL HARRISON

W
FRANKLIN WATTS
LONDON • SYDNEY

First published in 2014 by Franklin Watts

Copyright © Arcturus Holdings Limited

Franklin Watts
338 Euston Road
London NW1 3BH

Franklin Watts Australia
Level 17/207 Kent Street, Sydney NSW 2000

Produced by Arcturus Publishing Limited,
26/27 Bickels Yard, 151–153 Bermondsey Street, London SE1 3HA

Text: Paul Harrison
Editor: Joe Harris
Assistant editor: Frances Evans
Picture research: Mirco De Cet
Design: sprout.uk.com
Cover design: sprout.uk.com

Picture credits
Ariel Ltd: contents, 30, 31. Automobili Lamborghini: 8, 9. Corbis: 24 (Car Culture), 25 (Car Culture). ED Archives: 14, 15. Ford
of Britain: cover, 28, 29. Getty: 21. IFCAR: 5. Morgan Motor Co: 12b, 13t, 12-13. Noble Automotive Ltd: 22-23, 22t, 22b. OSX:
4-5. Porsche Cars Great Britain: 6-7. Shutterstock: 20t (Angyalosi Beata), 16t, 17 (Dongliu), 16b (Gustavo Fadel), 10-11 (Sam
Moores). Spyker Cars/The S3 Agency: 26-27.

A CIP catalogue record for this book is available from the British Library.

Dewey Decimal Classification Number 629.2'221

ISBN 978 1 4451 3230 3

Printed in China

Franklin Watts is a division of Hachette Children's Books, an Hachette UK company.
www.hachette.co.uk

SL004072UK

Supplier 29, Date 0514, Print run 3417

CONTENTS

FERRARI 458 ITALIA

What makes the Ferrari 458 an extreme supercar and one of the world's most desirable cars? Drop-dead good looks help, plus it can reach amazing speeds. In fact, the 458 Italia is one of the best supercars that money can buy. It's easy to spot one – just look for the crowd of admirers standing around taking photos!

You don't get a lot of frills for your money. If you want satnav or to connect your iPod inside the 458 you have to pay extra! There may not be many frills, but there are still plenty of thrills.

There is an open-top version of this car, too, called the 458 Spider. Even though it hasn't got a roof, it's actually more expensive than the Italia!

Owners can choose many different options for their car. They can even choose how wide they would like the stitching on the seats to be.

Ferrari has a proud car racing history, which is why its cars are traditionally red. This was the colour of Italian racing cars and Ferrari has kept the colour ever since.

Air vents near the front lights help to cool the brakes.

The 458 is known as a 'baby Ferrari', which means it is one of the smaller cars made by the company. It doesn't make it any less super though – it's actually faster than some of the larger Ferraris! And at a cost of £178,491 there's nothing babyish about its price tag.

The horse logo was first used in 1923 as a tribute to Francesco Barraca. He was an Italian World War I air force hero who used the prancing horse on his plane.

SUPER STATS

FERRARI 458 ITALIA
TOP SPEED: 325 km/h (202 mph)
0-100 KM/H (0-62MPH): 3.4 seconds
FUEL ECONOMY (COMBINED): 20.6 mpg
HORSEPOWER: 562 bhp
LENGTH: 4,527 mm (178.2 in)
WIDTH: 1,937 mm (76.3 in)
HEIGHT: 1,213 mm (47.8 in)
MADE IN: Italy
PRICE: £178,491

MEAN MACHINES

PORSCHE 911 CARRERA 4S

The Porsche 911 Carrera 4S is incredible – even by supercar standards – and that's because it's a supercar you can use every day. This might not sound too amazing, but usually when designers make a supercar they think about its looks first and then how useful it is. That's not the case with the 911, though – it's a dream to drive and there's even space for a suitcase. Very few supercars can compete with that.

Most of the car's body panels are made from aluminium, which is strong but very light. The lighter the car is, the faster it can go!

The first designs for the 911 were drawn by Ferdinand Porsche – the same man who designed the original Volkswagen Beetle!

The Carrera 4S version of the 911 is unusual for a Porsche as the engine power goes to all four wheels instead of just the rear wheels. This is a truly speedy 4x4!

Four-wheel drive helps the car to grip the road surface in wet conditions.

The driver can alter any aspect of the car's performance. Buttons adjust everything, from the gear box and how the car handles to the noise the exhaust makes.

The 911 is one of the longest lasting supercar models ever! The first 911 rolled off the production lines in 1963 and surprisingly the car's shape hasn't changed very much at all – perhaps the designers thought they'd got it right the first time.

Unlike most cars, the 911 has its engine at the back. This could cause the car to swing out on tight bends. However, the 911's excellent grip stops this from happening.

The designers of the Porsche 911 caused an outcry among fans when they decided to change the way the engine was cooled. They changed from air vents to a more standard water cooling method. That proves that this car is so super, no one wants anything to be changed!

SUPER STATS

PORSCHE 911 CARRERA 4S
TOP SPEED: 299 km/h (185 mph)
0-100 KM/H (0-62MPH): 4.5 seconds
FUEL ECONOMY (COMBINED): 28.5 mpg
HORSEPOWER: 400 bhp
LENGTH: 4,491 mm (176.8 in)
WIDTH: 1,852 mm (72.9 in)
HEIGHT: 1,296 mm (51.0 in)
MADE IN: Germany
PRICE: £88,493

LAMBORGHINI AVENTADOR

The Lamborghini Aventador is the ultimate supercar because it combines stunning good looks with powerful speed. It's hugely wide and incredibly low. And the noise from its massive V12 engine can be heard from the other end of town. This shouldn't bother Aventador owners though – if you drive a car like this, you probably enjoy all the attention.

Like most supercars, the Aventador only has two seats, which is bad news if you need to give more than one person a lift.

The Aventador is blisteringly quick – so fast, in fact, that the Dubai police force has bought one as a specialist pursuit vehicle. That should mean they can catch almost anyone else on the road. It also means they've got the coolest police car around.

The body of the Aventador is made from carbon fibre. Apart from being strong and light it will also never rust.

The body needs to be strong to stop it from twisting when the car goes round corners.

The Aventador has what are called 'scissor doors'. This describes the way they swing up and down to open and close.

Although famous for their supercars, Lamborghini actually started out by making tractors! The owner, Ferruccio Lamborghini, felt he had been insulted by the Ferrari car company. So he vowed to build cars that would put Ferrari in the shade. The Aventador is the latest in a long line of amazing cars that resulted from Ferruccio's decision.

Although the Aventador uses fuel like it's going out of fashion, it does try to be green (honestly!). Every time you stop, the engine switches off to save petrol. Then it starts again in just 180 milliseconds when you want to move on.

SUPER STATS

LAMBORGHINI AVENTADOR
TOP SPEED: 350 km/h (217 mph)
0-100 KM/H (0-62MPH): 2.9 seconds
FUEL ECONOMY (COMBINED): 16.4 mpg
HORSEPOWER: 700 bhp
LENGTH: 4,780 mm (188.2 in)
WIDTH: 2,265 mm (89.2 in)
HEIGHT: 1,136 mm (44.7 in)
MADE IN: Italy
PRICE: £247,668

ASTON MARTIN
V12 ZAGATO

Aston Martin, the creator of James Bond's car of choice, has been voted the coolest brand in the world six times since 2000! Its cars don't get any cooler than the V12 Zagato. This so-cool-it's-ice-cold car is made by Aston Martin and Italian company Zagato. The V12 proves these companies know how to make a beautiful supercar.

Aston Martin invented four new colour shades which are used on the Zagato and no other car.

It takes 100 hours to paint each car!

Zagato are 'coachbuilders', which means they make the bodies of cars for different companies. Zagato and Aston Martin have worked together for 50 years to make limited editions of Aston Martin cars.

Aston Martin will only make 101 of these cars, so they are bound to become collector's items.

The Zagato isn't really a new car at all. It's basically an Aston Martin Vanquish with a new body on top. And with a bigger price tag – it's well over £100,000 more expensive than a Vanquish!

When designing the car, Aston Martin tried out an early model on the racetrack in a proper competitive race – and won.

SUPER STATS

ASTON MARTIN V 12 ZAGATO
TOP SPEED: 305 km/h (190 mph)
0-100 KM/H (0-62MPH): 4.2 seconds
FUEL ECONOMY (COMBINED): 17.3 mpg
HORSEPOWER: 510 bhp
LENGTH: 4,385 mm (172.6 in)
WIDTH: 2,022 mm (79.6 in)
HEIGHT: 1,250 mm (49.2 in)
MADE IN: Great Britain
PRICE: £396,000

MORGAN AEROMAX

The Morgan Aero Coupe might look like it belongs on a 1930s film set, but it's actually one of today's most interesting supercars. It has a traditional design but uses very modern technology. The Aero Coupe might have jaw-dropping looks and blistering pace, but it's made slowly and with care – which makes it all the more desirable.

The sporty looking Aero Coupe is based on a Morgan racing car called the GT3 Aero.

Morgan doesn't make its own engines. The engine in the Aero Coupe comes from the German car makers BMW.

The interior of the car is trimmed with a hardwood called ash. This can be hand polished into different colours.

The large rear window makes it easy to park the Coupe – unlike most supercars!

Morgan cars might have modern-day technology, but they also use traditional car-making techniques. For example, the cars are hand built and customers can choose different colours and interiors to make their car unique. This all takes time though – so if you want one, you'd better be prepared to wait.

Morgan makes other cars that look even more old-fashioned than the Aero Coupe!

Designers used high-tech super formed aluminium panels for the entire body.

The car frame is made from aluminium too, as Morgan believes it gives a combination of lightness and strength.

SUPER STATS

MORGAN AERO COUPE
TOP SPEED: 273 km/h (170 mph)
0-100 KM/H (0-62MPH): 4.5 seconds
FUEL ECONOMY (COMBINED): 23 mpg
HORSEPOWER: 315 bhp
LENGTH: 4,147 mm (163 in)
WIDTH: 1,751 mm (68.9 in)
HEIGHT: 1,248 mm (49.1 in)
MADE IN: Great Britain
PRICE: £99,950

MCLAREN F1

The ultimate supercar combines show-stopping good looks with incredible speed. The McLaren F1 ticks both those boxes. McLaren runs a highly successful Formula 1 racing team, so it's no surprise to learn that when the company made a road car called the F1, it was the fastest on the market. Twenty years later, it's still one of the fastest cars on the road and it's still good-looking enough to draw a crowd.

It took four years to design and build the F1.

The F1's engine bay was lined in gold foil because it reflected more of the heat produced by the V12 engine than any other material.

To keep the car's weight down, even the toolkit is made from titanium, a metal which is only half as heavy as steel.

The wheels are made from a magnesium alloy – McLaren's choice for strength and lightness.

Other supercars may have beaten the F1's record of world's fastest road car, but it's still one of the most desirable cars around. Only 64 of the road-going versions were ever made, so getting hold of one can be tricky. When one does come up for sale, they aren't cheap. In 2012, an F1 was sold at auction for a staggering £3.5 million!

Although the F1 was a highly advanced car, it didn't have ABS, traction control or even power steering – all available on normal family cars.

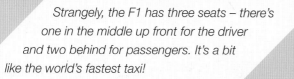

Strangely, the F1 has three seats – there's one in the middle up front for the driver and two behind for passengers. It's a bit like the world's fastest taxi!

SUPER STATS

MCLAREN F1

TOP SPEED: 386 km/h (240 mph)

0-100 KM/H (0-62MPH): 3.2 seconds

FUEL ECONOMY (COMBINED): 15.2 mpg

HORSEPOWER: 620 bhp

LENGTH: 4,288 mm (168.8 in)

WIDTH: 1,820 mm (71.7 in)

HEIGHT: 1,149 mm (45.2 in)

MADE IN: Great Britain

PRICE: £635,000 when new; £3.5 million + at auction.

PAGANI HUAYRA

Supercars are meant to be exclusive – they're not everyday cars after all. Being exclusive also means that they're usually very expensive. But there aren't many that cost as much as the Pagani Huayra. At nearly £850,000 the Huayra is eye-wateringly expensive, but you do get an amazing car for your cash.

The weight of the car is almost perfectly balanced between the front and the back of the car. This makes for a car that handles excellently.

Every bolt in the Huayra is made from titanium and is stamped with the car company's name.

Over 4,000 different parts are used to make up the Huayra – and that doesn't include the engine or gearbox.

There are flaps that pop up at the front and back of the car. These help to press the car to the road and give the Huayra extra grip – especially round corners.

Pagani is a small Italian company – big enough to build brilliant cars, but not big enough to build everything itself. This means that it works with other companies that make parts like the brakes, the engine and the exhaust system. Of course, these are all made to the highest standard demanded by Pagani.

When the driver applies the brakes the special flaps pop up to help slow the car down. These flaps, called air brakes, are also used by aircraft!

No expense has been spared. Even the clocks inside the Huayra are made by Rolex, the luxury watch maker.

SUPER STATS

PAGANI HUAYRA
TOP SPEED: 362 km/h (225 mph)
0-100 KM/H (0-62MPH): 3.3 seconds
FUEL ECONOMY (COMBINED): 18.8 mpg
HORSEPOWER: 720 bhp
LENGTH: 4,605 mm (181.3 in)
WIDTH: 2,036 mm (80.2 in)
HEIGHT: 1,169 mm (46.0 in)
MADE IN: Italy
PRICE: £849,000

FISKER KARMA

The Fisker Karma is a different sort of supercar. For a start, it's got real room for rear passengers and four doors so they can get in and out easily. But the most amazing thing about the Karma is that it is partly powered by electricity, not just petrol. So it's a green supercar – you don't see many of those around!

The roof doubles as a solar panel, which generates enough electricity to power all the lighting and extends the distance, or range, that the car is able to travel.

The headlights use LED bulbs, which are bright and don't use much electricity.

Celebrities such as Usher and Justin Bieber own Fisker Karmas.

The biggest problem with electric cars is that they have a short range. If you drive too far, then the batteries run flat and you come to a stop. The Karma gets round this problem by having two engines in one. You can drive just using the electric motor, or with both petrol and electricity powering the car.

The Karma was designed by the same man who created the Aston Martin Vantage and the BMW Z8.

Electric cars don't make any sound, so the Karma makes a fake engine noise to warn people that it is approaching.

The only downside of the Karma is that having two power supplies makes it very heavy. However, that doesn't seem to affect the car's performance too much!

SUPER STATS

FISKER KARMA
201 KM/H (125 MPH)
TOP SPEED: 201 km/h (125 mph)
0-100 KM/H (0-62MPH): 6.3 seconds
FUEL ECONOMY (COMBINED): Not available
HORSEPOWER: 260 bhp
LENGTH: 4,998 mm (196.8 in)
WIDTH: 2,133 mm (84.0 in)
HEIGHT: 1,330 mm (52.4 in)
MADE IN: USA
PRICE: £87,000

Some of the wood used to make the dashboard and doors look smart is around 300 years old. What's more, the trees it came from were found sunk on the bottom of Lake Michigan!

BLOODHOUND SSC

If a supercar is meant to be super-quick and super-rare, then Bloodhound SSC must be the most super of them all. Not only is it aiming to be the fastest car of all time, it's also one of a kind – and you don't get any more rare than that!

Bloodhound doesn't have just one engine – it has three! A jet engine gets things going, a rocket engine takes it up to top speed and a race car engine keeps the power coming to the fuel pumps.

The jet engine is normally found on Eurofighter Typhoon airplanes.

There's no room for passengers – that's because there's just one seat!

The letters SSC in Bloodhound's name stand for 'supersonic car'. That's because Bloodhound has been designed to travel faster than the speed of sound. The speed at which sound travels depends on your altitude, but at ground level it measures 1,235 km/h (767 mph). Bloodhound aims to smash that figure and hit speeds of over 1,609 km/h (1,000 mph)!

The car will be driven by a jet fighter pilot called Andy Green. He also drove the car that holds the current land speed record, Thrust SSC.

Normal tyres on the wheels would fall apart at supersonic speeds. Instead, the wheels are made from solid aluminium.

Bloodhound will be travelling so quickly it will need three different types of brakes. It has normal wheel brakes, flaps that rise up called air brakes (which aircraft use) and parachutes.

The tall fin at the back helps keep the car pointing straight ahead.

SUPER STATS

BLOODHOUND SSC
TOP SPEED: Over 1,600 km/h (over 1,000 mph)
0-100 KM/H (0-62MPH): Unknown
FUEL ECONOMY (COMBINED): Not available
HORSEPOWER: 135,000 bhp
LENGTH: 13,470 mm (530.3 in)
WIDTH: 1,900 mm (74.8 in)
HEIGHT: 3,000 mm (118.1 in)
MADE IN: Great Britain
PRICE: Not for sale

EXTREME SUPERCARS

NOBLE M600

The Noble M600 is a rarity – a top level supercar that's not made by a gigantic car company. It is built by a small team of around twenty people on an industrial estate in Britain. The M600 might be a David against the Goliaths of the supercar world, but it does something different to set itself apart from its richer cousins.

The body is made of carbon fibre, which is very strong and light.

There are three different settings that alter the way the car handles. The driver can choose road, sport or race. Race is the fastest and road is the most comfortable.

The unique attraction of the M600 is that it's a really basic car – it's stripped back to the bare essentials. Other supercars have loads of fancy gizmos like paddle shift gears, electronic stability control and anti-lock brakes. The M600 ignores all of these. The idea is that the more basic the car is, the more the driver feels like they are involved with the journey – and plenty of people agree with that idea.

Each car has its own number printed on the dashboard and the names of the people who built it engraved on the door sill.

Japanese firm Yamaha makes the engine. The same one was used in a Volvo SUV – but this wasn't as fast as the Noble!

SUPER STATS

NOBLE M600
TOP SPEED: 362 km/h (225 mph)
0-100 KM/H (0-62MPH): 3.5 seconds
FUEL ECONOMY (COMBINED): 18 mpg
HORSEPOWER: 650 bhp
LENGTH: 4,360 mm (171.6 in)
WIDTH: 1,910 mm (75.2 in)
HEIGHT: 1,140 mm (44.8 in)
MADE IN: Great Britain
PRICE: £200,000

MERCEDES SLR STIRLING MOSS

The Mercedes SLR Stirling Moss looks like a racing car from the 1950s and that's entirely deliberate. Mercedes has a proud tradition of building racing cars. This extreme supercar is named after one of the company's most famous racing drivers. And just like the racing car, the SLR has race-winning performance figures too!

The body is made from carbon fibre.

The two air scoops behind the seats also act as roll bars, which protect the driver and passenger if the car should ever roll over.

An air brake on the boot lid lifts automatically to provide extra grip and slow the car down.

The SLR is meant to look similar to the Mercedes which Stirling Moss drove in the 1950s.

When there are no passengers a special cover, known as a tonneau cover, goes over the passenger seat.

There are four exhaust pipes, two on each side at the front of the car.

As well as being a supercar, the **Mercedes SLR Stirling Moss is super exclusive.** Apart from its amazing speed, it's also very rare. Just 75 of them were made and not just anyone could buy one. Not only is it staggeringly expensive but potential owners were hand-picked by Mercedes. The company decided that only existing owners of Mercedes SLR cars would be able to buy one!

This Mercedes is a more basic version of their SLR range, a more run-of-the-mill supercar – if such a thing exists!

You don't get a lot for your money. There's no stereo, satnav, roof or even a windscreen, so you have to wear goggles when you drive it.

SUPER STATS

MERCEDES SLR STIRLING MOSS
TOP SPEED: 349 km/h (217 mph)
0-100 KM/H (0-62MPH): 3.5 seconds
FUEL ECONOMY (COMBINED): 8 mpg
HORSEPOWER: 641 bhp
LENGTH: 4,656 mm (183.3 in)
WIDTH: 1,908 mm (75.1 in)
HEIGHT: 1,281 mm (50.4 in)
MADE IN: Germany
PRICE: £660,000

SPYKER C8 AILERON

Countries such as Italy, Britain and Germany are well known for making supercars. But Spyker makes some of the most unusual and exciting cars on the planet and the company comes from a country that is not as famous for motoring. Spyker is based in the Netherlands and its C8 Aileron shows that the Dutch can make a supercar as well as anyone else!

The Spyker has a 'rear diffuser'. This uses the air travelling under the car to pull the car more tightly to the road and improve handling.

The air inlets on the roof and on the sides of the car are shaped like jet engines.

The wheels are meant to look like the blades in a jet turbine engine.

Spyker cars are hand-built.

Spyker used to make aircraft back in the early days of plane flight... and you can tell. The gear lever rods are left open to view as in an early plane instead of being hidden away. It has an aircraft-style ignition (starter) switch. 'Aileron' is the name given to a movable flap on the wing of an airplane and Spyker describes the place where the driver sits as the 'cockpit' and it being under the 'canopy' rather than the 'cabin' and the 'roof'.

The body panels and frame are made from aluminium.

The Spyker logo on the front of the bonnet is an old-fashioned propeller. That's because Spyker made fighter planes during World War I.

Aileron owners can order matching luggage made especially for Spyker by luxury bag maker Louis Vuitton – but it costs an extra £17,800. Those are some expensive bags!

SUPER STATS

SPYKER C8 AILERON

TOP SPEED: 300 km/h (187 mph)
0-100 KM/H (0-62MPH): 4.5 seconds
FUEL ECONOMY (COMBINED): 17 mpg
HORSEPOWER: 400 bhp
LENGTH: 4,618 mm (181.8 in)
WIDTH: 1,953 mm (76.9 in)
HEIGHT: 1,270 mm (50.0 in)
MADE IN: Netherlands
PRICE: £194,000

FORD GT

It's a strange fact that some of the world's most expensive supercars have been made by some of the smallest companies. And some of the biggest brands don't really make much of an effort when it comes to supercars. Take the Ford motor company, for example – it's huge, but the only supercar it has made in the last forty years is the GT. It was worth the wait though!

The driver presses a red button on the dashboard to start the engine.

The original GT40 was a successful racing car for Ford.

Unlike most supercars, the GT is easy to drive at low speeds. Often, supercars feel heavy and are difficult to steer.

Inside, the GT is a mixture of metal and a lightweight plastic and fibreglass mix called Azdel composite. Motorhomes also use Azdel composite, which perhaps makes the GT feel less special than it should!

One of the problems of supercars is their ridiculous width. TV presenter Jeremy Clarkson discovered this to his cost when his GT got stuck on Hammersmith Bridge in London because it was too wide!

The fuel tank is in the middle of the car to try and spread the weight evenly and to protect the tank in a crash.

Big, wide tyres provide lots of grip.

The GT looks very similar to Ford's only other supercar, the GT40, which it built after falling out with Ferrari. That's the second time Ferrari has annoyed someone so much they go off and build a Ferrari-beating car. You would think they would have learned from the first time!

SUPER STATS

FORD GT
TOP SPEED: 341 km/h (212 mph)
0-100 KM/H (0-62MPH): 3.7 seconds
FUEL ECONOMY (COMBINED): 14.6 mpg
HORSEPOWER: 550 bhp
LENGTH: 4,643 mm (182.8 in)
WIDTH: 1,953 mm (76.9 in)
HEIGHT: 1,125 mm (44.3 in)
MADE IN: USA
PRICE: £126,000

ARIEL ATOM 3.5

Supercar buyers expect their vehicles to be filled with cutting-edge technology and to be made from the world's most up-to-date materials. That's not quite the case with the Ariel Atom, though, where the idea seems to be that less is more. The Atom doesn't have a roof, windscreen, doors or even body panels!

This air intake at the back also protects the driver in a crash.

The atom uses a Honda i-VTEC engine. The Japanese car-maker has made over 13 million of these engines and not one of them has failed!

The Atom has won competitions for the fastest car to accelerate from 0 to 160 km/h (100 mph) and to return to 0 km/h (0 mph).

Although driving an Atom is like driving a Formula 1 racing car unlike the racer, the Atom has a seat for a passenger.

Ariel started out by making Penny Farthing bicycles back in the late 1800s. Although these bikes look strange to us today, at the time they were actually racing bikes. Ariel has continued to make sports vehicles ever since, from early grand prix cars and motor bikes to their present model, the Atom 3.5.

The chassis of the car wraps round the driver and passenger to offer them some protection.

Although the Atom's engine is quite small, the car is still really quick thanks to its super-light weight.

Owners can buy a windscreen as an option if they want one – but most don't bother.

SUPER STATS

ARIEL ATOM 3.5
TOP SPEED: 249 km/h (155 mph)
0-100 KM/H (0-62MPH): 2.7 seconds
FUEL ECONOMY (COMBINED): Not known
HORSEPOWER: 310 bhp
LENGTH: 3,410 mm (134.2 in)
WIDTH: 1,828 mm (72.0 in)
HEIGHT: 1,195 mm (47.0 in)
MADE IN: Great Britain
PRICE: £30,000

MEAN MACHINES

GLOSSARY

ABS This stands for 'Anti-lock Braking System', which slows cars down safely.

air scoop An opening in the car's bonnet or hood that enables air to flow in and cool the engine.

aluminium A lightweight metal.

bhp This stands for 'brake horsepower', and is a measurement of the engine's power.

carbon fibre A strong, light material made from thin rods of carbon. Carbon is also found in coal and diamonds.

chassis The base of a motor vehicle.

fibreglass A covering material that is made from glass fibres.

magnesium alloy A mixture of magnesium and other metals.

mpg This stands for 'miles per gallon'. It means the distance a car can travel using one gallon of fuel.

performance figures Measurements that show how well a car works.

titanium A shiny white metal that does not rust easily.

turbine engine A type of engine in which a wheel is turned by water, gas or steam to create continuous power.

FURTHER READING

Daynes, Katie. *Racing Cars* (Beginners Plus). Usborne, 2011.

Editors of DK. *Car Crazy.* Dorling Kindersley, 2012.

Hammond, Richard. *Car Science.* Dorling Kindersley, 2011.

Master, Matt. *Top Gear: 100 Fastest Cars*. BBC Children's Books, 2011.

Parker, Steve. *How It Works: Cars, Trucks and Bikes.* Miles Kelly, 2009.

INDEX